Thin Places

Thin Places

A Six-Week Prayer Guide for Experiencing God in Your Everyday Life

KEITH RILEY
Art Created by Katelyn Dixon

RESOURCE *Publications* · Eugene, Oregon

THIN PLACES
A Six-Week Prayer Guide for Experiencing God in Your Everyday Life

Copyright © 2024 Keith Riley. All rights reserved. Except for brief quotations in critical publications or reviews, no part of this book may be reproduced in any manner without prior written permission from the publisher. Write: Permissions, Wipf and Stock Publishers, 199 W. 8th Ave., Suite 3, Eugene, OR 97401.

Resource Publications
An Imprint of Wipf and Stock Publishers
199 W. 8th Ave., Suite 3
Eugene, OR 97401

www.wipfandstock.com

PAPERBACK ISBN: 979-8-3852-2890-4
HARDCOVER ISBN: 979-8-3852-2891-1
EBOOK ISBN: 979-8-3852-2892-8
VERSION NUMBER 12/05/24

The Scripture quotations contained herein are from the New Revised Standard Version Bible, copyright 1989 by the Division of Christian Education of the National Council of the Churches of Christ in the U.S.A. Used by permission. All rights reserved.

To my daughter, Amaya, may the work of my life help you to know that you are beloved, and that the wellspring of Love is within you and around you, always.

Contents

Acknowledgments | ix
Introduction | xi

Week 1: God—The Loving Trinity | 1
Week 2: You are Sacred | 17
Week 3: Sacredness of Creation | 33
Week 4: God in the Sacred Ordinary | 49
Week 5: Humans are Sacred | 65
Week 6: Sacred Rhythms | 81

Acknowledgments

There are many people who have spoken into me and thus spoken into this work. The guidance and teaching of Colette Cross, John Ortberg, Nathan Foster, Mimi Dixon, Trevor Hudson and MaryKate Morse are woven in every word that I write or speak. I can never fully express my gratitude for how they have impacted and shaped my life.

Katelyn Dixon is a wonderful leader, and I deeply admire her ability to see God within writing, art, poetry, and places of creativity. She partnered with me to create the artwork within this guide, and I'm grateful for her heart and friendship. To see the images in color go to www.sacredthinplaces.com.

I also want to thank Sam Littlefield, Grace Pouch, and Becca Smith for reading and giving insight into the shaping of my words and this guide in various stages.

Introduction

In Celtic tradition, there is a concept known as 'thin places.' These are locations that are said to be sacred because the veil between heaven and earth is thin. Over the years, these places have become travel destinations for people searching to communicate more clearly with God and thus are seen as having a deep sense of sacredness. One Celtic saying said, "Heaven and earth are only three feet apart, but in thin places, that distance is even shorter." This saying reflects the Celtic Christian belief that God is always close to them and can be seen in all aspects of creation. You can find God's reflection and presence in trees, rivers, songs, or a special friend. All creation is seen as sacred. As you begin to use this guide, I hope these concepts inspire you to discover the thin places all around you.

It might be best to find a consistent spot to sit each time you engage with this guide; allow this space to be unique to what is most helpful for you. It should be comfortable and free of distractions if possible. If you love to be outdoors, then be outdoors. If you have a favorite comfy chair in your home, be there. Have a candle close by if that helps center you or make a cup of coffee to enjoy. You may find that you have a thin place right in your own home, and I hope you come to discover that you yourself are a thin place. That inside your soul is the unique place where God is as close as your breath and speaking to you. I hope you find the truth that you are sacred.

Each week of the guide will move you through a different theme to help you begin to see the thin places all around you. Week one will begin with helping us contemplate our view of God and how

INTRODUCTION

it may need healing or expansion. During week two, we reflect on our image of self and our status as God's beloved. In Week three, we look around at the wonders of creation so that we can more clearly see the Creator. Week four is designed to help you see that your ordinary normal life is sacred, full of God's divine love, and better understand how we hold the reality of brokenness and evil around us. Week five will examine the sacredness of the people all around you. Then to close, Week six will allow us to sit within some key concepts that help us establish prayer within our rhythms of life. The hope of this guide is that it will lead to growth in prayer practices that will help you build new rhythms of listening to God within your daily life.

Our First Steps into Prayer

What is prayer? Prayer is where our inner desires and longings meet the welcoming love of God. It's the expression of the relationship between us and God. In prayer, we can communicate the hopes and desires for our lives now and for those that we love. The focus of prayer is union with God. God desires to draw us into the eternal flowing relationship of the Trinity and to be formed by this divine love. True prayer shapes us deeper into this image of love for the sake of the world around us. In prayer, we are reminded that we are the beloved of God.

How does prayer work? Prayer has many forms, and we will practice different methods of prayer in this guide. The essentials of prayer are to open yourself up to something beyond you. We are open to God speaking to us in written words, words spoken by others, nature, our inner voice, imaginations, music, art and so much more. God is ready to communicate with us, but we must learn to have an openness and awareness towards God. Which is why this guide has been crafted to help you grow in openness and awareness of God's presence with you.

Each week will serve as a guide into a deeper theme of understanding God, your own sacredness and the invitations of God all

Introduction

around you. In the guide, you will find each week is made up of five days of practice, one day of rest, and one day for reflection with community. For the five days of practice each week, you will find each day structured with these four components:

Slow: This is a section for you to slow down from the fast speed of your day and settle into God's loving presence with you. This section will guide you to enter into silence and pay attention to your body in the space by relaxing or taking a deep breath. Feel the freedom to slow down and be relaxed.

Meditate: The meditate section is designed to help you thoughtfully consider the themes of the weeks such as how you view God, yourself, the earth, or others around you. You may find these thoughts new or familiar, and hopefully will sit with you as you move into your day. This short paragraph is designed to help you think about the week's theme and sets up the next section of reflection questions.

Reflect: Here, there will be questions that help you consider how the mediation reflection interacts with your life. Spend time here and consider the questions with God. Listen deeply inside yourself and ponder what God might be trying to show you. Don't rush, and feel free to write down thoughts that are stirring within you.

Praxis: The praxis is a prayer practice for you to take into your day that will reinforce the theme from your prayer time into your ordinary rhythms. There is an old Latin saying that reads, "Repetition is the mother of all learning," and I believe that repeating these praxes will help you find the ones that help you the most. Each week will have you repeating a practice throughout the week, and this is intentional to help you apply this practice to your life.

Embracing Solitude and Meditation

Solitude and meditation are two key components that are needed in order to take further steps into prayer, even though these may

Introduction

not be part of your normal rhythms of life. Below are brief introductory paragraphs for each concept.

Meditation

In Christian meditation, we aim to settle ourselves deeper into God's love and Jesus' way of life. In some forms of meditation, the aim is to empty and detach. When we consider how to meditate as Christians, it should be in the framework of moving deeper into connection with God like a branch to a vine. Jesus talks about our need for union in this way in John 15:4–5, "Abide in me as I abide in you. Just as the branch cannot bear fruit by itself unless it abides in the vine, neither can you unless you abide in me. I am the vine, you are the branches. Those who abide in me and I in them bear much fruit, because apart from me you can do nothing." As you make space to meditate on love, you begin to understand that God's love is not far away or beyond you, but as near to you as the breath in our lungs. This opens us to the inner wellspring of love deep within that allows you to love yourself, God and other humans more fully.

Solitude

We live in a distracted world. We are constantly bombarded or overwhelmed by the noise and demands of the world around us. Attention spans continue to decline because we are constantly flooded by information and technology that is coming towards us at a torrent rate. Smartphones particularly are a wonderful gift that help us in life, but they have also become a part of our bodies. Some people have problems detaching completely from their phone for even a few minutes at a time. In solitude, we learn to slow down and remove these many distractions. This helps us listen to what is going on inside of ourselves and to create space to hear God's voice. Solitude can be a difficult practice to cultivate because we feel the urge to hurry, be productive, and be entertained. In this

Introduction

space, we also encounter our inner fears and scars, but God invites us into the quiet to be immersed in love. In solitude, we can rest in God's presence and know that we are loved just as we are in that moment. When we move into this practice it helps to form us into people who love ourselves, love others, and love God. Solitude is a great practice to help us reconnect with God in the natural world as well. Where we learn to low ourselves from the haste of our human endeavors and rest in the love of the Creator as we immerse ourselves in the beautiful creation.

"A person who is silent and still can hear the faintest whisper of God's voice in the rustling of the leaves and the flowing of the stream."—St. Columba of Iona

Practical Helps

- Find a journal or some way to write down your thoughts and reflections as you move through the guide. This helps you process where God is meeting you in your times of prayer.
- Be comfortable. As often as you can, have your prayer in the same space that feels natural and safe for you with relatively minimal distractions.
- If you are able, have someone with you to process this journey of prayer. This could mean you do this guide with someone else or have a spiritual director or friend to talk about your experiences along the way. You can also journey with a small group of friends for encouragement and dialogue. At the end of each week, you will find a resource for reflecting and praying with your group.
- Set the time in your calendar and try to use the guide at the same time each day. This will help you remember and establish consistent rhythms in your day-to-day life.

Week 1: God—The Loving Trinity

Week 1—Day 1—God is Love

Slow

Relax your body into your space and take a deep breath. Be aware of God near you.

"As the Father has loved me, so I have loved you; abide in my love."—John 15:9

Meditate

On our first day, our invitation is to settle into the reality that God is love. God is an endless circle of love and belonging known as the Trinity. When Jesus was asked to summarize how God wants us to live, he stated that we should love God and love others as ourselves (see Matthew 22:37–39). Love is central because God is an unending fountain of love that sustains all we know and see. But often, the primary image of God we have been given is a wrathful God who is angry at us for our sins. God does get angry and upset at injustice and evil, and we should be glad for those images of bringing justice and restoration. However, the avenue of how God relates to us is through openness and love. God loves you and is pursuing you in love today.

"God's love is a guiding light, leading us through the darkness of this world to the eternal embrace of God's presence."—St. Aidan of Lindisfarne

Reflect

Slowly read 1 John 4:16 *"And so we know and rely on the love God has for us.*

God is love. Whoever lives in love lives in God, and God in them."

Reread the verse and take note of any word or phrase that stands out to you.

How have you known love in your life?

What do you imagine God's posture is towards you?

Praxis

Daily prayer practices are designed to be invitations for you to grow in your awareness of God with you in your day. Take the practice below and experiment with it in your daily routine.

BREATH PRAYER

Pause during the day and take a few deep breaths. As you breathe in, imagine you are breathing in God's love, and as you breathe out, imagine releasing your anxieties and worries. Between each breath, you can say, "God loves me". This is called a breath prayer and can help center you into God's loving presence with you.

Week 1—Day 2—God is Near

Slow

Relax your body into your space and take a deep breath. Be aware of God with you.

"Peace be with you. As the Father has sent me, so I send you." When he had said this, he breathed on them and said to them, "Receive the Holy Spirit."—John 20:21–22

Meditate

Take a deep breath in and out. God is near to you as that breath. The comforting stories that Jesus gave his disciples as he prepared to leave them all centered around God being with them. He prayed they would be as connected to God as a vine to a branch. He prayed for them to have union with God just as he had demonstrated in his life. Jesus spoke of God's Spirit being with them and guiding them. Then, after the resurrection, Jesus appeared to the disciples and breathed on them. This breath is the Spirit of God coming upon the disciples. This imagery calls back to the first pages of the Bible. God makes humans and breathes into them to give their bodies life. Paul uses the language "in Christ" more than any other phrase to talk about the wonderful life of union that we live with God now. As you are wondering if God is near and with you, breathe in and breathe out, God is near.

Reflect

What emotions/thoughts/questions arise as you think of God being near?

Is it an easy or difficult thought to imagine God with you in your ordinary day?

Praxis

Daily prayer practices are designed to be invitations for you to grow in your awareness of God with you in your day. Take the practice below and experiment with it in your daily routine.

Breath Prayer

Pause during the day and take a few deep breaths. As you breathe in, imagine you are breathing in God's love, and as you breathe out, imagine releasing your anxieties and worries. Between each breath, you can say, "God loves me". This is called a breath prayer and can help center you into God's loving presence with you.

Week 1—Day 3—God is Feminine and Masculine

Slow

Relax your body into your space and take a deep breath. Be aware of God with you.

"Humankind was created as God's reflection: in the divine image God created them; female and male, God made them." Genesis 1:27

"As a mother comforts her child, so I will comfort you"—Isaiah 66:13

"Then Jesus took a little child and put it among them; and taking it in his arms, he said to them, "Whoever welcomes one such child in my name welcomes me, and whoever welcomes me welcomes not me but the one who sent me."—Mark 9:36-37

Meditate

A large majority of Christians that grew up in the church imagine God as exclusively male and only use male language to speak of God. However, according to Christian theology, God or the Trinity is beyond gender. Yes, the historical Jesus was a human, Jewish male, but the fullness of the Trinity represents both the feminine and masculine. All of humankind was made in the image of God, both female and male. There is feminine and masculine imagery throughout the biblical text of God, from God being a mother (giving birth, nursing, protecting) to being a loving father (listens, gift giver). This is helpful for some of us and unsettling for others, but this opens us to the reality that the feminine is sacred. Too often, even in the church, women have been treated less than men. Women are image bearers of God just as men are image bearers. For all of us to draw close to God, we must feel safe with God, and God is ready for you to draw near. Whether that means you move towards God with the imagery of Mother, Father, suffering Jewish man, spirit, or light, take a step into God's safe embrace.

Reflect

How do you feel knowing you are made in the image of God?

What image or metaphor of God brings you peace?

Praxis

Breath Prayer

Pause during the day and take a few deep breaths. As you breathe in, imagine you are breathing in God's love, and as you breathe out, imagine releasing your anxieties and worries. Between each breath, you can say, "God loves me". This is called a breath prayer and can help center you into God's loving presence with you.

Week 1—Day 4—God's Character

Slow

Relax your body into your space. Take a deep breath. Be aware of God with you.

"Love is patient; love is kind; love is not envious or boastful or arrogant or rude. It does not insist on its own way; it is not irritable or resentful; it does not rejoice in wrongdoing, but rejoices in the truth. It bears all things, believes all things, hopes all things, endures all things."—1 Corinthians 13:4–7

Meditate

When we have a conversation with someone, their tone and character shape how we receive that conversation. If someone is patient, warm, and compassionate towards us, we feel safe and open to that person. If someone is hurried, cold, and distant, we tend not to feel a connection with that person or want to be near them. This brings us to ask, as you approach God, what tone does God use with you, and what is God's character? Remembering that the Bible teaches us that God is love, reread the verses from 1 Corinthians with God in place of the word love.

"God is patient; God is kind; God is not envious or boastful or arrogant or rude. God does not insist on God's own way; God is not irritable or resentful; God does not rejoice in wrongdoing, but rejoices in the truth. God bears all things, believes all things, hopes all things, endures all things."

Reflect

What words stand out to you from the passage above? Why?

How would you describe God's voice?

Praxis

BREATH PRAYER

Pause during the day and take a few deep breaths. As you breathe in, imagine you are breathing in God's love, and as you breathe out, imagine releasing your anxieties and worries. Between each breath, you can say, "God loves me". This is called a breath prayer and can help center you into God's loving presence with you.

Week 1—Day 5—God is Unhurried

Slow

Relax your body into your space. Take a deep breath. Be aware of God with you.

"Be still, and know that I am God."—Psalm 46:10

Meditate

The world often moves at what feels like a frantic pace, and we often find ourselves pulled along into that speed of hurry. Sometimes, it feels good to be in a hurry. It speaks to our desires to be needed and to matter. These are good desires, but hurry does not speak deeply into them. Hurry does violence to the present moment of time. We get in a rush to move to the next thing and keep on the schedule. Slowly, this shifts our attention away from the moment right in front of us. Jesus was never in a hurry (read Mark 5:21–43 to see a story of an unhurried Jesus). Jesus stayed present in each moment before going on to the next. This allowed him to see each person in healing ways. Jesus saw people's feelings and desires. Everyone mattered to him, and he was able to demonstrate great love by simply being. God does not need you to hurry and impress. You can simply be. Be present in God's unhurried love.

Reflect

What feelings does it give you to go slowly?

How can you practice being unhurried in your life?

Praxis

BREATH PRAYER

Pause during the day and take a few deep breaths. As you breathe in, imagine you are breathing in God's love, and as you breathe out, imagine releasing your anxieties and worries. Between each breath, you can say, "God loves me". This is called a breath prayer and can help center you into God's loving presence with you.

Week 1—Day of Rest

Each week, you will have a day of rest set into your rhythms. This is to give you space for reflection and to find soul rest in God. Use the prompt below to live into the theme that you have been exploring within the frameworks of meditation and solitude.

Create space in your day to relax with God. You could choose to relax by taking a nap, going for a walk, gardening, reading a good novel, enjoying your favorite coffee shop, etc. The key is to pick something that brings you joy and feels life-giving to you. Trust that as you relax, God is with you and delights in you enjoying some space to recharge. God created you and knows you enjoy relaxing in this way. At some point, use your imagination to see God smiling at you.

Reflection Questions

Where did you interact with God?

Was there a praxis that brought you joy this week?

What emotions and thoughts come to you as you imagine God delighting in you?

Visio Divina

Use the artwork to spend time in prayer with God. Pay attention to what you notice in the image from colors, shapes or style. Ask God what you should see in this image. Prayerfully listen for God's stirring and promptings while you engage with the art.

What do you notice about the image?

What emotions does it evoke?

Week 1—Group Reflection

Welcome to your group reflection for the week. Each week, you will use the following format to listen and hold each other's journeys with God. We offer the gift of our listening to each other and ask that what is said in this space stays here. This gives us the freedom to share openly and honestly about our journeys. We are not here to fix anyone manage impressions, or act as guides. We are here to listen to each other and to listen to God. Choose one person each week to facilitate your time and rotate throughout the guide.

Slow

Facilitator: Relax your body into your space and take a deep breath. Be aware of God with you.

Spend a few minutes centering into the silence and God's presence with you.

When ready, the facilitator can read the prayer below to bring your group together from the silence:

Blessed Trinity,

Your beloved children are here.

Open our ears and hearts to each other.

Help us to hear you.

Guide us in your love.

Amen.

Week 1: God—The Loving Trinity

Meditate and Reflect

Facilitator: Take a few minutes to reflect on the week silently. You can look over your notes as you think about how you met with God in prayer this week. Use this question as a prompt as needed: What meditation or praxis helped you to connect with God? Why?

Praxis

After everyone has had time to reflect, open the group to a time of sharing where each member has space to speak uninterrupted as they are ready. Take turns and go slow. We have plenty of time to listen. Remember that as each person shares, the rest of the group should listen in complete silence without comments or questions and hold that person dearly in their heart before God.

Facilitator: We open this space for someone to share.

First Person Sharing: Whoever feels led to begin can share from their reflections. Remember that this is a time to share about your journey into prayer from the week. This could be about the practices, meditations, or some other way you experienced God.

After the first sharing, thank the person for sharing and return to silent prayer for a few minutes, holding the person and their words before God.

Facilitator: As we are listening to God, is there something that you want to share with _____?

Keep in mind that this is not a time to coach, give advice or tell your story. Pray over what you might say and speak from simplicity an image, verse, word, etc. that God gives you. Use your discernment, not everyone needs to share.

When the responses are over, the facilitator asks: May we pray for you aloud?

Then repeat the process until everyone has had the opportunity to share.

Week 2: You are Sacred

Week 2—Day 1—Made in the Image of God

Slow

Relax your body into your space. Take a deep breath. Be aware of God with you.

"Then God said, "Let us make humankind in our image, according to our likeness" . . .

So God created humankind in his image, in the image of God he created them; male and female he created them."—Genesis 1:26, 27

Meditate

The first pages of the Bible tell the story of creation. We can all agree with statements about the sea, mountains, light, stars, and animals being called 'good' by God. We still wonder in awe at these things today! Yet, interestingly, humans are the centerpiece of the story. They are made in the image of God, and it's when they're created that God calls everything 'very good.' When we look at ourselves or other people around us, sometimes we forget that we are looking at fellow image-bearers of God. Evil and darkness have marred us, and in our wounded state, it is easy to forget that what is truest of us is good, beautiful, and in God's image. The church has at times moved too heavily into shame/guilt-based narratives around salvation and reduced our view of ourselves as primarily a sinner. Yet, what is truest in you is beautiful, good, and in the image of God. You are beautiful and good, no matter the scars and wounds you carry. You are made in the image of God, and you are his Beloved.

Reflect

How has your understanding of yourself grown or shifted in recent years?

What do you think about being made in the image of God?

Praxis

Prayer of the Beloved

Place your hands on your chest and hold them there for this prayer. This physical action simulates the feeling of being hugged. Take a few deep breaths. Imagine God lovingly holding you and saying, "You are my beloved." Repeat this as many times as you need.

Now imagine seeing yourself and saying, "You are beloved. You are loved." Repeat this as many times as you need, and imagine giving yourself a hug.

End by saying out loud, "I am God's beloved. I am loved."

Week 2—Day 2—Sacred Soul

Slow

Relax your body into your space. Take a deep breath. Be aware of God with you.

"As the Father has loved me, so I have loved you; abide in my love."—John 15:9

"As God's chosen ones, holy and beloved, clothe yourselves with compassion, kindness, humility, meekness, and patience."—Colossians 3:12

Meditate

You are sacred. Say this out loud, "I am sacred." It is a beautiful truth of Christianity that all humans are sacred, no matter if we believe the right things or act in accordance with specific rules. We are all sacred beings with eternal destinies. This word sacred simply means being connected to God. Yet, amid a broken world, we quickly forget that reality when we look in the mirror. Jesus guides us in the path of accepting that we are God's beloved. He teaches us how to live within that love as the source of life. We do not need to do anything or earn our way to this status which at times can feel counterintuitive to many of us. You are simply sacred and beloved for being you. The invitation is to accept that and find healing, grace, and wholeness of self in the way of Jesus.

Reflect

What emotions do you feel when thinking about being sacred?

What do you think hinders people from viewing themselves as sacred?

Praxis

Prayer of the Beloved

Place your hands on your chest and hold them there for this prayer. This physical action simulates the feeling of being hugged. Take a few deep breaths. Imagine God lovingly holding you and saying, "You are my beloved." Repeat this as many times as you need.

Now imagine seeing yourself and saying, "You are beloved. You are loved." Repeat this as many times as you need, and imagine giving yourself a hug.

End by saying out loud, "I am God's beloved. I am loved."

Week 2—Day 3—Flourishing Life Now

Slow

Relax your body into your space. Take a deep breath. Be aware of God with you.

"Therefore be imitators of God, as beloved children, and live in love, as Christ loved us and gave himself up for us, a fragrant offering and sacrifice to God."—Ephesians 5:1–2

Meditate

When we think about God or spirituality, there is a tendency to mainly think about an afterlife. A common question asked by evangelists is, "Where would you go?" Yet, what Jesus offers us is a vibrant life within God's love right here, right now. Jesus teaches that living within God's shalom (peace and wholeness) is available to us and opens a whole new dimension of life. Jesus models for people how to live by following his way of life or becoming his disciples. This doesn't mean we no longer have problems or will instantly become wealthy, but rather we learn to live out of a place of love. Love that feels like home and transforms us.

Reflect

How does it feel to know that God cares about your everyday life?

Spend some time reflecting on what you consider to be elements of a flourishing life.

Praxis

Prayer of the Beloved

Place your hands on your chest and hold them there for this prayer. This physical action simulates the feeling of being hugged. Take a few deep breaths. Imagine God lovingly holding you and saying, "You are my beloved." Repeat this as many times as you need.

Now imagine seeing yourself and saying, "You are beloved. You are loved." Repeat this as many times as you need, and imagine giving yourself a hug.

End by saying out loud, "I am God's beloved. I am loved."

Week 2—Day 4—Loving Yourself

Slow

Relax your body into your space. Take a deep breath. Be aware of God with you.

"When you regarded me

Your eyes imprinted your grace in me,

In this, you loved me again,

And thus my eyes merited

To also love what you see in me...

Let us go forth together to see ourselves in Your beauty."

- St. John of the Cross

Meditate

God's love transforms us. It reshapes our understanding of the world and how we see ourselves. It is easy to look in the mirror and not love everything we see. We know the things that lie beneath the surface, such as regrets, disappointments, mistakes, and fears. These things can quickly warp and cloud our view of self to the point that we may not be able to see ourselves clearly. God made you with your unique gifts, skills, passions, appearance, voice, and inner spirit. You are uniquely made in love. We can live from our true selves by God's grace and transformative work in us.

Reflect

What unique traits or qualities about yourself make you proud?

Reflect on loving yourself and where that may be difficult for you.

Praxis

Prayer of the Beloved

Place your hands on your chest and hold them there for this prayer. This physical action simulates the feeling of being hugged. Take a few deep breaths. Imagine God lovingly holding you and saying, "You are my beloved." Repeat this as many times as you need.

Now imagine seeing yourself and saying, "You are beloved. You are loved." Repeat this as many times as you need, and imagine giving yourself a hug.

End by saying out loud, "I am God's beloved. I am loved."

Week 2—Day 5—Holding Our Brokenness

Slow

Relax your body into your space. Take a deep breath. Be aware of God with you.

"He heals the brokenhearted, and binds up their wounds."—Psalm 147:3

Meditate

At times, life can, feel as if it is full of disappointments and pain. We may have experienced situations that have caused us to feel broken or deep wounds from the past that are still painful to recall. These traumas leave their mark upon our souls, haunting with shame or guilt, and can make us wonder if we are worthy of love. The good news of Jesus is that these broken spaces within us can receive the love of God. Some of these wounds might not be fully healed in this life, but they do not have to leave us in darkness and despair. Christ sits with us in our tears and brokenness as one who experienced tears and brokenness in his own life. He does not cast more guilt or shame, but instead looks upon us with love, kindness, and gentleness. When we can look at our brokenness, accept it, and gently place it in Christ's hands, only then we can continue down the path of healing. The path where God is holding our brokenness with us and gently whispering, "You are loved; you are my beloved child."

Reflect

What current or recent pains do you need to gently hold before God?

What practices have you found helpful for healing?

Praxis

PRAYER OF THE BELOVED

Place your hands on your chest and hold them there for this prayer. This physical action simulates the feeling of being hugged. Take a few deep breaths. Imagine God lovingly holding you and saying, "You are my beloved." Repeat this as many times as you need.

Now imagine seeing yourself and saying, "You are beloved. You are loved." Repeat this as many times as you need, and imagine giving yourself a hug.

End by saying out loud, "I am God's beloved. I am loved."

Week 2—Day of Rest

As you enter your day of rest, remember that this is to give you space for reflection and to find soul rest in God. Hold the themes from these first two weeks in your heart—that the Loving Trinity is near you and that you are sacred and loved by God.

Create space in your day to relax with God. You could choose to relax by taking a nap, going for a walk, gardening, reading a good novel, enjoying your favorite coffee shop, etc. The key is to pick something that brings you joy and feels life-giving to you. Trust that as you relax, God is with you and delights in you enjoying some space to recharge. God created you and knows that you enjoy relaxing in this way. At some point, use your imagination to see God smiling at you.

Reflection Questions

Where did you interact with God?

Was there a praxis that brought you joy this week?

What activities or practices bring you joy and life?

Visio Divina

Use the artwork to spend time in prayer with God. Pay attention to what you notice in the image from colors, shapes or style. Ask God what you should see in this image. Prayerfully listen for God's stirring and promptings while you engage with the art.

What do you notice about the image?

What emotions does it evoke?

Week 2—Group Reflection

Welcome to your group reflection for the week. Each week, you will use the following format to listen and hold each other's journeys with God. We offer the gift of our listening to each other and ask that what is said in this space stays here. This gives us the freedom to share openly and honestly about our journeys. We are not here to fix anyone manage impressions, or act as guides. We are here to listen to each other and to listen to God. Choose one person each week to facilitate your time and rotate throughout the guide.

Slow

Facilitator: Relax your body into your space and take a deep breath. Be aware of God with you.

Spend a few minutes centering into the silence and God's presence with you.

When ready, the facilitator can read the prayer below to bring your group together from the silence:

Blessed Trinity,

Your beloved children are here.

Open our ears and hearts to each other.

Help us to hear you.

Guide us in your love.

Amen.

Week 2: You are Sacred

Meditate and Reflect

Facilitator: Take a few minutes to silently reflect on the week. You can look over your notes as you think about how you met with God in prayer. Use this question as a prompt as needed: What meditation or praxis helped you to connect with God? Why?

Praxis

After everyone has had time to reflect, open the group to a time of sharing where each member has space to speak uninterrupted as they are ready. Take turns and go slow. We have plenty of time to listen. Remember that as each person shares, the rest of the group should listen in complete silence without comments or questions and hold that person dearly in their heart before God.

Facilitator: We open this space for someone to share.

First Person Sharing: Whoever feels led to begin can share from their reflections. Remember that this is a time to share about your journey into prayer from the week. This could be about the practices, meditations, or some other way you experienced God.

After the first sharing, thank the person for sharing and return to silent prayer for a few minutes, holding the person and their words before God.

Facilitator: As we are listening to God, is there something that you want to share with _____?

Keep in mind that this is not a time to coach, give advice or tell your story. Pray over what you might say and speak from simplicity an image, verse, word, etc. that God gives you. Use your discernment, not everyone needs to share.

When the responses are over, the facilitator asks: May we pray for you aloud?

Then repeat the process until everyone has had the opportunity to share.

Week 3: Sacredness of Creation

Week 3—Day 1—God Revealed in Creation

Slow

Relax your body into your space. Take a deep breath. Be aware of God with you.

"Ever since the creation of the world his eternal power and divine nature, invisible though they are, have been understood and seen through the things he has made."—Romans 1:20

Meditate

Have you ever been completely in awe of nature? Maybe it was a stunning sunset at the beach or perhaps a beautiful mountain view that still lives in your memory. Our own neighborhoods can fill us with wonder with the sights of flowers, hummingbirds, or a majestic old tree. The complexity that is within a simple flower or wings of a butterfly can stay with you for days. Followers of Jesus have long talked about the two great books of revelation in which we are able to know God more deeply, the book of scripture and the book of creation. We too often forget about the gift of creation and the way it points us towards our Creator. Our first step is to begin to see the invitation of God all around us in creation.

Reflect

What place in nature helps you to relax and feel wonder?

How can you cultivate space in your schedule to be in nature?

Praxis

PRAYER OF ATTENTION

Find space in your day to sit outside in a place you enjoy (this could be your backyard, favorite park, or nature path). Say this simple prayer: "Blessed Creator, help me pay attention to your creation and grow in wonder of you." Look around you and find something to pay attention to and examine. Ask God to help you notice new things. Use all of your senses and take your time. Find joy in discovering the wonder of creation God has made for you to enjoy.

Week 3—Day 2—God in Light and Darkness

Slow

Relax your body into your space. Take a deep breath. Be aware of God with you.

"What has come into being in him was life, and the life was the light of all people. The light shines in the darkness, and the darkness did not overcome it."—John 1:3–5

"The true light, which enlightens everyone, was coming into the world."—John 1:9

Meditate

Are you afraid of the dark? Most adults would quickly say no, but children often fear dark spaces and the monsters looming inside them. We may still have fears of the dark, but we know how to turn on the lights. Light gives us clarity and vision so that we can see and understand the world around us more vividly. This is true in our physical world and the interior spaces of our hearts and minds. Darkness does not need to be only viewed as unknown and scary, but as a place for rest and dependency. We sleep in the dark, which is why Celtic Christians would pray compline (or evening protection prayer). In the night, we are asleep and vulnerable, but the darkness reminds us to trust and depend upon the Light. Read this poem slowly as you begin to reflect upon the peace given in the light.

A candle flickered in the breeze

Darkness settled in for the night

Shapes and shadows loomed about

Confusing and menacing in the dark

Then in the soft revealing light aglow

I saw them clearly without fear

In the light, peace is revealed

Reflect

Where are you seeking light or guidance in your life?

Reflect on the concept of being dependent upon God. Where in your life does this feel simple and where does it feel complicated?

Praxis

PRAYER OF ATTENTION

Find space in your day to sit outside in a place you enjoy (this could be your backyard, favorite park, or nature path). Say this simple prayer: "Blessed Creator, help me pay attention to your creation and grow in wonder of you." Look around you and find something to pay attention to and examine. Ask God to help you notice new things. Use all of your senses and take your time. Find joy in discovering the wonder of creation God has made for you to enjoy.

Week 3—Day 3—Beauty of Creation

Slow

Relax your body into your space. Take a deep breath. Be aware of God with you.

"Let the heavens be glad, and let the earth rejoice;

Let the sea roar, and all that fills it;

Let the field exult, and everything in it.

Then shall all the trees of the forest sing for joy."- Psalm 96:11–12

"You are the author of beauty."—Wisdom 13:3

Meditate

Beautiful sites evoke something deep within us. We understand this when we find something beautiful in art or music, but especially within nature itself. People travel to see beautiful natural sites like the Grand Canyon, Hawaiian beaches, or the Swiss Alps. There is a universal desire to witness beauty, and God speaks to us in the midst of it. Scripture reminds us that "every generous act of giving, with every perfect gift, is from above, coming down from the Father of lights" (James 1:17) and God has designed us to delight in the perfect gift of creation. As a parent watches their children play and enjoy life, God looks at us with delight when we are enjoying the great beautiful gift of creation.

"Everybody needs beauty as well as bread, places to play in and pray in, where nature may heal and give strength to body and soul alike."—John Muir

Reflect

What is a beautiful location that you have memories of visiting? Why do you think that you remember it so vividly?

What do you find beautiful in nature? How could you rhythmically create space to be near this beauty in nature?

Praxis

PRAYER OF ATTENTION

Find space in your day to sit outside in a place you enjoy (this could be your backyard, favorite park, or nature path). Say this simple prayer: "Blessed Creator, help me pay attention to your creation and grow in wonder of you." Look around you and find something to pay attention to and examine. Ask God to help you notice new things. Use all of your senses and take your time. Find joy in discovering the wonder of creation God has made for you to enjoy.

Week 3—Day 4—Care of Creation

Slow

Relax your body into your space. Take a deep breath. Be aware of God with you.

"The whole earth is full of your glory."—Isaiah 6:3

Meditate

As Christians, part of our call to discipleship is to steward the creation around us. All of creation belongs to God, and God cares about how we use and treat the earth. This is not just about taking care of God's creation but also loving our neighbor as ourselves. What we do in the world impacts others' well-being and generations after us, and so if we are to love others well, we must learn to better care for our environments and create systems that highlight our interconnectedness. John Muir once said, "When one tugs at a single thing in nature, you find it attached to the rest of the world." We live in union with the trees, oceans, atmosphere, animals and all that God has created.

Reflect

What would caring for creation look like in your life?

What spiritual disciplines could help you cultivate care for creation?

Praxis

PRAYER OF ATTENTION

Find space in your day to sit outside in a place you enjoy (this could be your backyard, favorite park, or nature path). Say this simple prayer: "Blessed Creator, help me pay attention to your creation and grow in wonder of you." Look around you and find something to pay attention to and examine. Ask God to help you notice new things. Use all of your senses and take your time. Find joy in discovering the wonder of creation God has made for you to enjoy.

Week 3—Day 5—The Senses

Slow

Relax your body into your space. Take a deep breath. Be aware of God with you.

"All things came into being through him, and without him not one thing came into being."- John 1:3

Meditate

God made humans to experience the richness and fullness of life through our senses. Whether you go and watch a sunset or gaze upon the ocean's vastness or pick out your favorite flowers or smell fresh bread wafting out of the local bakery. The taste of your favorite slice of pizza or how you can experience love through a home-cooked meal made just for you. You pull that favorite soft, fluffy blanket over your skin or run your hand under cold flowing water. The sound of the voice of a loved one or the beat of your favorite song. God meets us in our senses, and these moments are doorways for us to see the connection of heaven and earth all around us.

Reflect

What would you say are some of your favorite smells or tastes?

Do you have a recent vivid memory of using your senses and being in awe of the experience?

Praxis

Prayer of Attention

Find space in your day to sit outside in a place you enjoy (this could be your backyard, favorite park, or nature path). Say this simple prayer: "Blessed Creator, help me pay attention to your creation and grow in wonder of you." Look around you and find something to pay attention to and examine. Ask God to help you notice new things. Use all of your senses and take your time. Find joy in discovering the wonder of creation God has made for you to enjoy.

Week 3—Day of Rest

Create space in your day to relax in nature with God in the practice of solitude. If you are able, go somewhere that you find relaxing within nature. This could be at your favorite hiking trail, a grove of your favorite trees, a nearby beach, or a favorite local park or nature conservatory. If you aren't sure where to go, search for a new place to go to explore near you. Maybe you will find a new favorite nature spot! The key is to pick a place that brings you joy and feels life-giving to you. Trust that as you relax in nature, God is with you and delights in you enjoying the wonders of creation. God created you and all that you see.

"All the wild world is beautiful, and it matters but little where we go, to highlands or lowlands, woods or plains, on the sea or land or down among the crystals of waves or high in a balloon in the sky; through all the climates, hot or cold, storms and calms, everywhere and always we are in God's eternal beauty and love. So universally true is this, the spot where we chance to be always seems the best."—John Muir

Reflection Questions

Where did you interact with God?

Was there a praxis that brought you joy this week?

What area of nature brings you peace? What type of rhythm could you introduce in your life to immerse yourself in that area of nature as part of your routine?

Visio Divina

Use the artwork to spend time in prayer with God. Pay attention to what you notice in the image from colors, shapes or style. Ask God what you should see in this image. Prayerfully listen for God's stirring and promptings while you engage with the art.

What do you notice about the image?

What emotions does it evoke?

Week 3—Group Reflection

Welcome to your group reflection for the week. Each week, you will use the following format to listen and hold each other's journeys with God. We offer the gift of our listening to each other and ask that what is said in this space stays here. This gives us the freedom to share openly and honestly about our journeys. We are not here to fix anyone manage impressions, or act as guides. We are here to listen to each other and to listen to God. Choose one person each week to facilitate your time and rotate throughout the guide.

Slow

Facilitator: Relax your body into your space and take a deep breath. Be aware of God with you.

Spend a few minutes centering into the silence and God's presence with you.

When ready, the facilitator can read the prayer below to bring your group together from the silence:

Blessed Trinity,

Your beloved children are here.

Open our ears and hearts to each other.

Help us to hear you.

Guide us in your love.

Amen.

Week 3: Sacredness of Creation

Meditate and Reflect

Facilitator: Take a few minutes to silently reflect on the week. You can look over your notes as you think about how you met with God in prayer. Use this question as a prompt as needed: What meditation or praxis helped you to connect with God? Why?

Praxis

After everyone has had time to reflect, open the group to a time of sharing where each member has space to speak uninterrupted as they are ready. Take turns and go slow. We have plenty of time to listen. Remember that as each person shares, the rest of the group should listen in complete silence without comments or questions and hold that person dearly in their heart before God.

Facilitator: We open this space for someone to share.

First Person Sharing: Whoever feels led to begin can share from their reflections. Remember that this is a time to share about your journey into prayer from the week. This could be about the practices, meditations, or some other way you experienced God.

After the first sharing, thank the person for sharing and return to silent prayer for a few minutes, holding the person and their words before God.

Facilitator: As we are listening to God, is there something that you want to share with _____?

Keep in mind that this is not a time to coach, give advice or tell your story. Pray over what you might say and speak from simplicity an image, verse, word, etc. that God gives you. Use your discernment, not everyone needs to share.

When the responses are over, the facilitator asks: May we pray for you aloud?

Then repeat the process until everyone has had the opportunity to share.

Week 4: God in the Sacred Ordinary

Week 4—Day 1—Your Sacred Everyday

Slow

Relax your body into your space. Take a deep breath. Be aware of God with you.

Meditate

Nothing reminds us of our ordinary, routine life like a Monday morning. The alarm goes off before we want to wake up, breakfast is a rush, there's traffic on the way to work, emails are piled up, and that work we put off from last week is waiting for us. Most of our days are spent not in any extraordinary scene but instead in normal uneventful days that, if we can learn to see, are full of God's presence and other sacred image bearers all around us. Living within God's kingdom means that we start to see that the world is permeated with God's presence and love. We learn that prayer is the way to connect to God as our source of life and guidance. Psalm 1 reminds us that when we live in this way with God, we "are like trees planted by streams of water, which yield their fruit in its season, and their leaves do not wither." This is the beautiful, ordinary, sacred life that we are invited to live into each morning.

Reflect

Think about a typical day in your life. Where is it easy to see God within your day? Why?

Where is it difficult to see God within your day? Why?

Praxis

Prayer in my Ordinary

As you begin your daily tasks today, say this prayer to increase your awareness of God with you in your everyday tasks:

"God, thank you for being with me while I _____ (do the dishes, respond to email, take a walk, etc). Help me to be aware of your love near me in this task."

Take a deep breath and be open to seeing how God is near you in the ordinary.

Week 4—Day 2—God in the Dishes and Vacuuming

Slow

Relax your body into your space. Take a deep breath. Be aware of God with you.

"Lord of all pots and pans and things, make me a saint by cooking meals and washing up the plates."—Brother Lawrence

Meditate

Our lives are full of ordinary tasks that we must do repeatedly. There is not a lot that feels sacred about the laundry, cleaning the dishes, vacuuming, mowing the grass, brushing our teeth, or paying the bills. Yet, what if we started to view these moments as invitations to be aware of God's loving presence with us? Holding to what we learned from week one about God (that God is near you and loves you) can help us begin to see that our everyday tasks can become moments of resting our lives in God's love. In those quiet and simple moments, God is whispering overtures of love to us. There was a monk named Brother Lawrence who wrote a book in the 1600s called Practicing the Presence of God. Listen to his words about prayer in the midst of our normal routine and tasks, "The time of work does not with me differ from the time of worship; and in the noise and clatter of my kitchen, even while several people are at the same time calling out for different things, I commune with God in as great a tranquility as if I were upon my knees in prayer in the holiest cathedral of worship."

Reflect

What is one of your least favorite routine tasks? What would it look like to be aware of God in that task?

What do you think hinders you from seeing small moments of life as sacred?

Praxis

Prayer in my Ordinary

As you begin your daily tasks today, say this prayer to increase your awareness of God with you in your everyday tasks:

"God, thank you for being with me while I _____ (do the dishes, respond to email, take a walk, etc). Help me to be aware of your love near me in this task."

Take a deep breath and be open to seeing how God is near you in this task.

Week 4—Day 3- God Given Pleasures

Slow

Relax your body into your space. Take a deep breath. Be aware of God with you.

"Go, eat your bread with enjoyment, and drink your wine with a merry heart; for God has long ago approved what you do."—Ecclesiastes 9:7

Meditate

We are made to enjoy the pleasures of life. The church has not always done a good job of celebrating this and, at times, has taught that our bodies can't be trusted, and all pleasures are bad. Yet, if we hold that God created us, then we realize God made us to have on average 3,000 taste buds on our tongues to detect different flavors. Our brains are wired to release dopamine to send signals to our bodies that we enjoy that food, thrill, sexual experience, dancing to your favorite song, shopping, or winning your favorite game. While the Bible gives us guidelines around these pleasures (centered around the commandment to love your neighbor as yourself, so that your pleasures do not take advantage of another human), we can also clearly see that God made us to enjoy the pleasures of our bodies, minds, and souls.

Reflect

Make a list of things that bring you pleasure and joy. Give thanks for each of the ways God has made you to enjoy pleasure.

Praxis

Prayer in my Ordinary

As you begin your daily tasks today, say this prayer to increase your awareness of God with you in your everyday tasks:

"God, thank you for being with me while I _____ (do the dishes, respond to email, take a walk, etc). Help me to be aware of your love near me in this task."

Take a deep breath and be open to seeing how God is near you in the ordinary.

Week 4—Day 4—God in our Suffering

Slow

Relax your body into your space. Take a deep breath. Be aware of God with you.

"When Jesus saw her weeping, and the Jews who came with her also weeping, he was greatly disturbed in spirit and deeply moved. He said, "Where have you laid him?" They said to him, "Lord, come and see." Jesus began to weep." John 11:33-35

Meditate

In the mystery of the incarnation, God dwells in humanity. God knows what it is like to trip and fall. God knows what it is like to enjoy the taste of food. God knows what it is like to run and jump. God knows what it is like to be sick. God knows what it is like to cry and grieve. Jesus lost his father before his earthly ministry ever started. We see Jesus weep at the death of Lazarus. Jesus was betrayed by his friends. Jesus was physically tortured and murdered. God knows what it is like to suffer. God is not the orchestrator of suffering, but He is instead the one who knows suffering, sits with us in it, and promises that it won't be the end. Resurrection is coming, but our pain and suffering is still real and difficult. How is God with us in our suffering? It could be the peace that comes in a meditation on love. It could be through the help of a counselor or therapist. It could be in the companionship of close friends and family. It could be that God is in our tears. In times of suffering, we can remember what Jesus told his friends on the night that he suffered, "I will not leave you orphaned" or alone, but the Helper will be with you.

Reflect

What has been your experience of God's presence in suffering?

Write out a lament to God about things that you are grieving or suffering you see. When you finish, read out loud your lament and imagine Jesus crying over the pain with you.

Praxis

PRAYER IN MY ORDINARY

As you begin your daily tasks today, say this prayer to increase your awareness of God with you in your everyday tasks:

"God, thank you for being with me while I _____ (do the dishes, respond to email, take a walk, etc). Help me to be aware of your love near me in this task."

Take a deep breath and be open to seeing how God is near you in the ordinary.

Week 4—Day 5—Loneliness

Slow

Relax your body into your space. Take a deep breath. Be aware of God with you.

"I will not leave you orphaned; I am coming to you."—John 14:18

Meditate

There are times in our lives when we feel isolated and alone. This may be an outward reality of our friendships and relationships being disconnected or broken, but it can also be a reality of our inner life. Although our world is connected like never before in history with the use of social media and technological advances, people report feeling alone and lonely at alarming rates. This reflects an inner loneliness and longing to truly be seen, understood, known, and loved. We often look for love far outside of ourselves and miss the invitation to move deep into an inner love. Cultivating an inner love for ourselves that finds its source in the love that God has placed deep within us can help us navigate moments of loneliness so that as we find those outer relationships, we are never tempted to make them the source of our life. We keep our center in the never fading love of God and let it radiate into all that we love. We will all face loneliness, but may we remember in those moments that God is near to us.

Reflect

How would you express the differences between solitude and loneliness?

How have you faced loneliness in your life?

Praxis

Prayer in my Ordinary

As you begin your daily tasks today, say this prayer to increase your awareness of God with you in your everyday tasks:

"God, thank you for being with me while I _____ (do the dishes, respond to email, take a walk, etc). Help me to be aware of your love near me in this task."

Take a deep breath and be open to seeing how God is near you in the ordinary.

Week 4—Day of Rest

Each week, you will have a day of rest set into your rhythms. This is to give you space for reflection and to find soul rest in God. Use the prompt for each week to live into the theme for the week.

Create space in your day to relax with God in your neighborhood. If you are able, go somewhere that you find relaxing within nature, a grove of favorite trees, neighborhood coffee shop, favorite local park, or your own home. If you aren't sure where to go then search for a new place to explore near you. Maybe you will find a new favorite nature spot in your own neighborhood! The key is to pick a place that brings you joy and feels life-giving to you. Trust that as you relax in your neighborhood, God is with you and delights in you enjoying the wonders of your ordinary life. God created you and all that you see. God delights in you. You are God's beloved.

Reflection Questions

Where did you interact with God?

Was there a praxis that brought you joy this week?

How does it feel that God cares and is present in your everyday life?

Visio Divina

Use the artwork to spend time in prayer with God. Pay attention to what you notice in the image from colors, shapes or style. Ask God what you should see in this image. Prayerfully listen for God's stirring and promptings while you engage with the art.

What do you notice about the image?

What emotions does it evoke?

Week 4—Group Reflection

Welcome to your group reflection for the week. Each week, you will use the following format to listen and hold each other's journeys with God. We offer the gift of our listening to each other and ask that what is said in this space stays here. This gives us the freedom to share openly and honestly about our journeys. We are not here to fix anyone manage impressions, or act as guides. We are here to listen to each other and to listen to God. Choose one person each week to facilitate your time and rotate throughout the guide.

Slow

Facilitator: Relax your body into your space and take a deep breath. Be aware of God with you.

Spend a few minutes centering into the silence and God's presence with you.

When ready, the facilitator can read the prayer below to bring your group together from the silence:

Blessed Trinity,

Your beloved children are here.

Open our ears and hearts to each other.

Help us to hear you.

Guide us in your love.

Amen.

Week 4: God in the Sacred Ordinary

Meditate and Reflect

Facilitator: Take a few minutes to silently reflect on the week. You can look over your notes as you think about how you met with God in prayer. Use this question as a prompt as needed: What meditation or praxis helped you to connect with God? Why?

Praxis

After everyone has had time to reflect, open the group to a time of sharing where each member has space to speak uninterrupted as they are ready. Take turns and go slow. We have plenty of time to listen. Remember that as each person shares, the rest of the group should listen in complete silence without comments or questions and hold that person dearly in their heart before God.

Facilitator: We open this space for someone to share.

First Person Sharing: Whoever feels led to begin can share from their reflections. Remember that this is a time to share about your journey into prayer from the week. This could be about the practices, meditations, or some other way you experienced God.

After the first sharing, thank the person for sharing and return to silent prayer for a few minutes, holding the person and their words before God.

Facilitator: As we are listening to God, is there something that you want to share with _____?

Keep in mind that this is not a time to coach, give advice or tell your story. Pray over what you might say and speak from simplicity an image, verse, word, etc. that God gives you. Use your discernment, not everyone needs to share.

When the responses are over, the facilitator asks: May we pray for you aloud?

Then repeat the process until everyone has had the opportunity to share.

Week 5: Humans are Sacred

Week 5—Day 1—Sacred Neighbor

Slow

Relax your body into your space. Take a deep breath. Be aware of God with you.

"He answered, "You shall love the Lord your God with all your heart, and with all your soul, and with all your strength, and with all your mind; and your neighbor as yourself.""—Luke 10:27

Meditate

Every human is sacred and marked by the divine image of God. It is easy for us to forget when we are moving through life and passing by people every day who we may or may not ever know. The reality of life is that your neighbor whom you wave to each day, the barista at your coffee shop, or the couple whom you always see out on a walk together are made in the image of God. They do not have to believe certain things about God or act in a certain way to be sacred and loved. They simply are because they are human. God loves them and calls us to love each person we meet. Jesus teaches this in his memorable parable of the Good Samaritan (see Luke 10:25–37). Each face you see today is the face of a sacred human being in which the image of God resides.

Reflect

Read Luke 10:25–37

How might holding this reality change your interactions today?

What do you feel stirring in your heart as you think about the parable of the Good Samaritan?

Praxis

BLESSING PRAYER FOR OTHERS

"God, help me to hear you in each person who speaks to me today and to see you in the eyes of each person who looks at me."

Repeat this prayer in your heart today. As often as you can, remember that everyone you encounter is an image-bearer of God, even though we are all broken and marred. Bless these persons with your attention, focus, and kindness through your interactions.

Week 5—Day 2—Sacred Enemy

Slow

Relax your body into your space. Take a deep breath. Be aware of God with you.

"Love your enemies and pray for those who persecute you."—Matthew 5:44

Meditate

Do you have any enemies? It may not be a typical question we ask ourselves, and many of us might quickly say, "No! Of course not!". Yet, if we examine the way that we are shaped to view the world, we might realize that we have many faceless enemies. These could be people on the other side of the political spectrum, people that are taking jobs/housing, fans of that other sports team, etc. Our world has fractured and divided us into camps and drawn targets on our enemies. Yet, Jesus implores us to pray for our enemies, to turn the other cheek, and to move in love towards all people. The way of the kingdom of God is radically different from the way of all other kingdoms of our world. Your "enemy" is a sacred image-bearer of God. God loves your enemies, even those who think radically differently than you. The transformation of our world does not come from the sword and hate but rather through radical, sacrificial love.

Reflect

What does the word 'enemy' bring up for you? What feelings arise as you think about God loving your enemies every bit as much as he loves you?

How could you practice 'loving your enemy' in your life?

Praxis

Blessing Prayer for Others

"God, help me to hear you in each person who speaks to me today and to see you in the eyes of each person who looks at me."

Repeat this prayer in your heart today. As often as you can, remember that everyone you encounter is an image-bearer of God, even though we are all broken and marred. Bless these persons with your attention, focus, and kindness through your interactions.

Week 5—Day 3—Spiritual Friendships

Slow

Relax your body into your space. Take a deep breath. Be aware of God with you.

"Bear one another's burdens, and in this way you will fulfill the law of Christ."—Galatians 6:2

Meditate

There is a deep longing inside of us to be seen and known. We can see this in the way children on a kindergarten playground form friendships and respond to the question, "Can I play with you?" We are made for community and companionship in life. We see this in our view of God as the Trinity being an eternal community of love between Father, Son, and Holy Spirit. We each have people in our lives that God has brought alongside our path to help us see ourselves more clearly. In return, we form unique spiritual friendships that shape our development as humans and mold us into people of God. In the Celtic tradition, a spiritual friend is called an Anam Cara. This is someone who knows the depths of our souls and becomes a companion on the joint pilgrimage deeper into the heart of God as we live into the way of Jesus. You probably can name some of these people whom you feel like God brought into your life at just the right time. Although these friends may not even live close in proximity to us, they always feel near to our souls.

Reflect

Who are your spiritual friends?

How have friendships helped you to grow in your spiritual formation?

Praxis

BLESSING PRAYER FOR OTHERS

"God, help me to hear you in each person who speaks to me today and to see you in the eyes of each person who looks at me."

Repeat this prayer in your heart today. As often as you can, remember that everyone you encounter is an image-bearer of God, even though we are all broken and marred. Bless these persons with your attention, focus, and kindness through your interactions.

Week 5—Day 4—Sacred Unseen

Slow

Relax your body into your space. Take a deep breath. Be aware of God with you.

"But seek the welfare of the city where I have sent you into exile, and pray to the Lord on its behalf."—Jeremiah 29:7

Meditate

One of the guiding commitments of being the people of God from the Old and New Testaments is to care for the poor, marginalized, and vulnerable. This could look like providing work for someone in need, caring for the poor with communal offerings, or selling personal property to step in the gap for a friend in debt. God cares about the details of our lives and the systems that make it more difficult for some due to where they were born or the color of their skin. Suffering exists in our world today because of war in their country, corrupt systems that are in place, racism, and misogyny. We are called as people of God to extend love, care, and provision for those whom are in our circles.

Reflect

How can you show up in your local community to care for those suffering or vulnerable?

Is there someone in your life who might feel unseen? How could you show them love?

Praxis

BLESSING PRAYER FOR OTHERS

"God, help me to hear you in each person who speaks to me today and to see you in the eyes of each person who looks at me."

Repeat this prayer in your heart today. As often as you can, remember that everyone you encounter is an image-bearer of God, even though we are all broken and marred. Bless these persons with your attention, focus, and kindness through your interactions.

Week 5—Day 5—Sacred World

Slow

Relax your body into your space. Take a deep breath. Be aware of God with you.

"You love all things that exist and hate nothing that you have made."—Wisdom 11:24

Meditate

There is nowhere we can go that has not been touched by the love of God. There is no person that you will see today who has not been formed by the love of God. There is no plant or animal that is not teeming with the life animating force of God. God holds our world in his hands, and it is saturated with his loving presence. Yes, there is evil and brokenness that has marred the world, but God's redemptive love is coming for the whole of creation. Paul says it this way in Romans 8:21, "that the creation itself will be set free from its bondage to decay and will obtain the freedom of the glory of the children of God." Our world is not something God will just throw away in the end, but it is destined for redemption. Our call is to be good stewards of this sacred space that God has given us to dwell in for such a time as this.

Reflect

Where do you see God's reflection in the world around you?

Praxis

BLESSING PRAYER FOR OTHERS

"God, help me to hear you in each person who speaks to me today and to see you in the eyes of each person who looks at me."

Repeat this prayer in your heart today. As often as you can, remember that everyone you encounter is an image-bearer of God, even though we are all broken and marred. Bless these persons with your attention, focus, and kindness through your interactions.

Week 5—Day of Rest

Create space in your day to relax with your favorite humans. If you are able, go somewhere that you can have fun and celebrate with those closest to you. If you aren't sure where to go, ask the friends or family that you are with what they would like to do. The key is to pick a place that brings you and those you love joy and feels life-giving. Trust that as you celebrate with those you love that God is with you and delights in all of you.

Reflection Questions

Where did you interact with God?

Was there a praxis that brought you joy this week?

How do you feel God calling you to invest in the sacred humans in your life?

Visio Divina

Use the artwork to spend time in prayer with God. Pay attention to what you notice in the image from colors, shapes or style. Ask God what you should see in this image. Prayerfully listen for God's stirring and promptings while you engage with the art.

What do you notice about the image?

What emotions does it evoke?

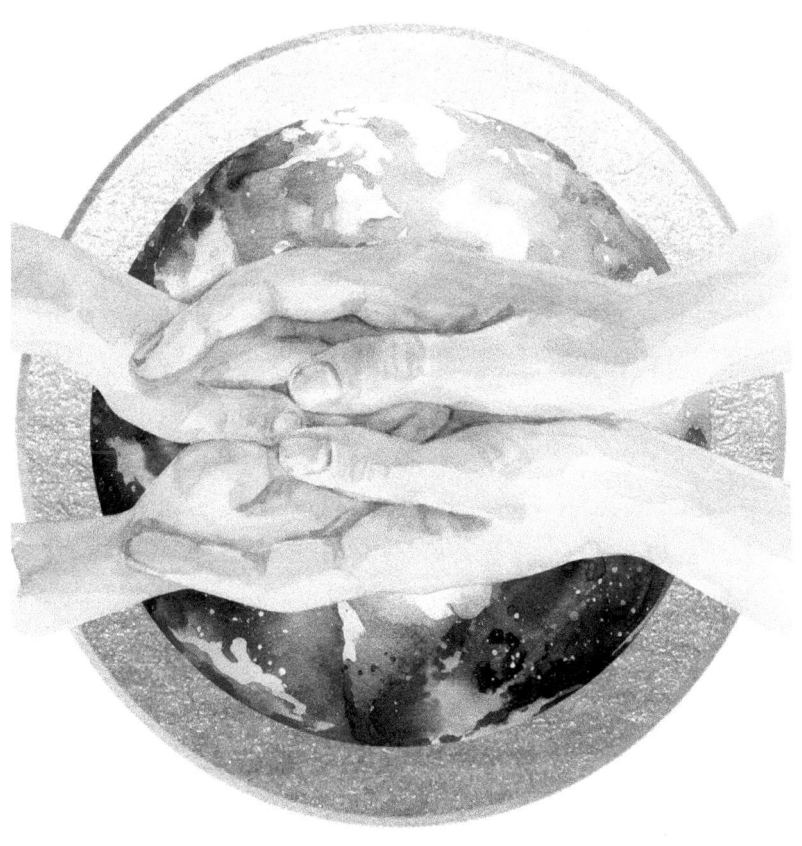

Week 5—Group Reflection

Welcome to your group reflection for the week. Each week, you will use the following format to listen and hold each other's journeys with God. We offer the gift of our listening to each other and ask that what is said in this space stays here. This gives us the freedom to share openly and honestly about our journeys. We are not here to fix anyone manage impressions, or act as guides. We are here to listen to each other and to listen to God. Choose one person each week to facilitate your time and rotate throughout the guide.

Slow

Facilitator: Relax your body into your space and take a deep breath. Be aware of God with you.

Spend a few minutes centering into the silence and God's presence with you.

When ready, the facilitator can read the prayer below to bring your group together from the silence:

Blessed Trinity,

Your beloved children are here.

Open our ears and hearts to each other.

Help us to hear you.

Guide us in your love.

Amen.

Week 5: Humans are Sacred

Meditate and Reflect

Facilitator: Take a few minutes to silently reflect on the week. You can look over your notes as you think about how you met with God in prayer. Use this question as a prompt as needed: What meditation or praxis helped you to connect with God? Why?

Praxis

After everyone has had time to reflect, open the group to a time of sharing where each member has space to speak uninterrupted as they are ready. Take turns and go slow. We have plenty of time to listen. Remember that as each person shares, the rest of the group should listen in complete silence without comments or questions and hold that person dearly in their heart before God.

Facilitator: We open this space for someone to share.

First Person Sharing: Whoever feels led to begin can share from their reflections. Remember that this is a time to share about your journey into prayer from the week. This could be about the practices, meditations, or some other way you experienced God.

After the first sharing, thank the person for sharing and return to silent prayer for a few minutes, holding the person and their words before God.

Facilitator: As we are listening to God, is there something that you want to share with _____?

Keep in mind that this is not a time to coach, give advice or tell your story. Pray over what you might say and speak from simplicity an image, verse, word, etc. that God gives you. Use your discernment, not everyone needs to share.

When the responses are over, the facilitator asks: May we pray for you aloud?

Then repeat the process until everyone has had the opportunity to share.

Week 6: Sacred Rhythms

Week 6—Day 1—Meditation

Slow

Relax your body into your space. Take a deep breath. Be aware of God with you.

"Happy are those who meditate on wisdom who reflect in their heart on her ways and ponder her secrets."—Ecclesiastes 14:20-21

Meditate

In Christian meditation, we aim to settle ourselves deeper into God's love and Jesus' way of life. In some forms of meditation, the aim is to empty and detach. When we consider how to meditate as Christians, it should be in the framework of moving deeper into connection with God like a branch to a vine. Jesus talks about our need for union in this way in John 15:4-5, "Abide in me as I abide in you. Just as the branch cannot bear fruit by itself unless it abides in the vine, neither can you unless you abide in me. I am the vine, you are the branches. Those who abide in me and I in them bear much fruit, because apart from me you can do nothing." As you make space to meditate on love, you begin to understand that God's love is not far away or beyond you, but as near to you as the breath in our lungs. This opens us to the inner wellspring of love deep within that allows you to love yourself, God and other humans more fully.

Reflect

What has the word meditate meant to you?

How has your understanding of meditation shifted while using this guide?

Praxis

PRAYER OF THE BELOVED

Place your hands on your chest and hold them there for this prayer. This physical action simulates the feeling of being hugged. Take a few deep breaths. Imagine God lovingly holding you and saying, "You are my beloved." Repeat this as many times as you need.

Now imagine seeing yourself and saying, "You are beloved. You are loved." Repeat this as many times as you need, and imagine giving yourself a hug.

End by saying out loud, "I am God's beloved. I am loved."

Week 6—Day 2—Solitude

Slow

Relax your body into your space. Take a deep breath. Be aware of God with you.

"After he dismissed the crowds, he went up the mountain by himself to pray."—Matthew 14:23

"For God alone my soul waits in silence, for my hope is from God."—Psalm 62:5

Meditate

We live in a distracted world. We are constantly bombarded or overwhelmed by the noise and demands of the world around us. Attention spans continue to decline because we are constantly flooded by information and technology that is coming towards us at a torrent rate. Smartphones particularly are a wonderful gift that help us in life, but they have also become a part of our bodies. Some people have problems detaching completely from their phone for even a few minutes at a time. In solitude, we learn to slow down and remove these many distractions. This helps us listen to what is going on inside of ourselves and to create space to hear God's voice. Solitude can be a difficult practice to cultivate because we feel the urge to hurry, be productive, and be entertained. In this space, we also encounter our inner fears and scars, but God invites us into solitude to be immersed in love. In solitude, we can rest in God's presence and know that we are loved just as we are in that moment. Solitude helps to form us into people who love ourselves, love others, and love God.

Reflect

What has your experience looked like in your time of solitude?

How could you introduce solitude into your daily rhythms? (For example, this could be a small amount in a day or a full day once a month)

Praxis

PRAYER OF ATTENTION

Find space in your day to sit outside in a place you enjoy (this could be your backyard, favorite park, or nature path). Say this simple prayer: "Blessed Creator, help me pay attention to your creation and grow in wonder of you." Look around you and find something to pay attention to and examine. Ask God to help you notice new things. Use all of your senses and take your time. Find joy in discovering the wonder of creation God has made for you to enjoy.

Week 6—Day 3—Beginning Again and Again

Slow

Relax your body into your space. Take a deep breath. Be aware of God with you.

"The Lord is my shepherd, I shall not want. He makes me lie down in green pastures; he leads me beside still waters." Psalm 23:1-2

Meditate

There is a common thread through most guides into prayer and the contemplative life, which is the fact that we are all still beginners in our life of prayer. Don't let this be a discouragement in any way but a gift in that none of us have arrived and become spiritual elite. Instead, we are all still students in the school of Jesus learning together. Jesus often invites people to come and see. I hope as you have been using this guide, you can feel Jesus gently inviting you deeper into beauty and presence to come and see what He wants to show and teach you. You may find that you want to journey in this guide again or pick up a new prayer book (Celtic Daily Prayer by the Northumbria Community is my favorite). Whatever the invitation you sense going forward, may you rest in the peace that you don't have to have it figured out and you are loved for who you are, not what you do.

Reflect

Where do you sense God's invitation drawing you deeper in this season of life?

What is something new that you learned in this prayer guide that you would like to steward/practice in your life?

Praxis

Prayer in my Ordinary

As you begin your daily tasks today, say this prayer to increase your awareness of God with you:

"God, thank you for being with me while I _____ (do the dishes, respond to email, take a walk, etc). Help me to be aware of your love near me in this task."

Take a deep breath and be open to seeing how God is near you in the ordinary.

Week 6—Day 4—Questions, Mystery and Paradox

Slow

Relax your body into your space. Take a deep breath. Be aware of God with you.

"For my thoughts are not your thoughts,

nor are your ways my ways, says the Lord.

For as the heavens are higher than the earth,

so are my ways higher than your ways

and my thoughts than your thoughts."—Isaiah 55:8–9

Meditate

God is beyond our reason and concrete answers. The concept of God as Trinity is a mystery in itself. Jesus in certain moments in his ministry confused his disciples and the crowds that listened to him. He would say things like 'to save your life, you must lose it' or 'the first will be last and the last shall be first'. Jesus taught with mystery and paradox. His primary response to questions asked of him was to ask a question in return. Jesus didn't lay out all the facts about God but instead slowly revealed fully the character of a loving God that had come to bring restoration, love, and healing. Your questions and doubts are welcomed by this God. He does not need you to believe all the right perfect things, but to accept the love that has been extended to you and to then learn to offer love to others.

Reflect

God can hold our questions and doubts. Write out what questions you want to ask God.

Praxis

Breath Prayer

Pause during the day and take a few deep breaths. As you breathe in, imagine you are breathing in God's love, and as you breathe out, imagine releasing your anxieties and worries. Between each breath, you can say, "God loves me". This is called a breath prayer and can help center you into God's loving presence with you.

Week 6—Day 5—Soul Friend

Slow

Relax your body into your space. Take a deep breath. Be aware of God with you.

"When David had finished speaking to Saul, the soul of Jonathan was bound to the soul of David, and Jonathan loved him as his own soul."—1 Samuel 18:1

Meditate

Friendship is a gift to us in life, but there are some special friendships that can be classified as spiritual friendships. These people see into our souls and allow us to be completely vulnerable within while feeling safe. These friendships are unique and special when we find them, because we have a sense that they are meant to be our friends in throughout this long journey. This person can be a family member or someone who simply feels like home. In Celtic tradition, this is known as an Anam Cara or Soul Friend. These friendships should be treasured for the depth of transformation that God can use this friend to bring into your life. They see us for who we are and call us to be our true selves. As you reflect on your life, maybe you have someone who is a soul friend for you. If so, reach out to them in gratitude for the gift of such friendship.

Reflect

Who is a soul friend for you?

What are your intentional rhythms for cultivating this friendship?

Praxis

Blessing Prayer for Others

"God, help me to hear you in each person who speaks to me today and to see you in the eyes of each person who looks at me."

Repeat this prayer in your heart today. As often as you can, remember that everyone you encounter is an image-bearer of God, even though we are all broken and marred. Bless these persons with your attention, focus, and kindness through your interactions.

Week 6—Day of Rest

Create space in your day to relax with God. If you are able, go somewhere that you have found in these last few weeks. Hopefully it is a new favorite spot! Again, the key is to pick a place that brings you joy and feels life-giving to you. Trust that as you relax in this place, God is with you and delights in how you engage and enjoy the wonders of creation and your ordinary life. Spend some time reflecting on your daily habits, environments, and the invitation from God into new sacred rhythms of prayer, rest, and reflection.

Reflection Questions

What praxis do you want to integrate into your daily rhythms?

Reflect on using this guide. What are you grateful for? What are your biggest takeaways?

Visio Divina

Use the artwork to spend time in prayer with God. Pay attention to what you notice in the image from colors, shapes, or style. Ask God what you should see in this image. Prayerfully listen for God's stirring and promptings while you engage with the art.

What do you notice about the image?

What emotions does it evoke?

Week 6—Group Reflection

Welcome to your group reflection for the week. Each week, you will use the following format to listen and hold each other's journeys with God. We offer the gift of our listening to each other and ask that what is said in this space stays here. This gives us the freedom to share openly and honestly about our journeys. We are not here to fix anyone manage impressions, or act as guides. We are here to listen to each other and to listen to God. Choose one person each week to facilitate your time and rotate throughout the guide.

Slow

Facilitator: Relax your body into your space and take a deep breath. Be aware of God with you.

Spend a few minutes centering into the silence and God's presence with you.

When ready, the facilitator can read the prayer below to bring your group together from the silence.

Blessed Trinity,

Your beloved children are here.

Open our ears and hearts to each other.

Help us to hear you.

Guide us in your love.

Amen.

Week 6: Sacred Rhythms

Meditate and Reflect

Facilitator: Take a few minutes to silently reflect on the week. You can look over your notes as you think about how you met with God in prayer. Use this question as a prompt as needed: What meditation or praxis helped you to connect with God? Why?

Praxis

After everyone has had time to reflect, open the group to a time of sharing where each member has space to speak uninterrupted as they are ready. Take turns and go slow. We have plenty of time to listen. Remember that as each person shares, the rest of the group should listen in complete silence without comments or questions and hold that person dearly in their heart before God.

Facilitator: We open this space for someone to share.

First Person Sharing: Whoever feels led to begin can share from their reflections. Remember that this is a time to share about your journey into prayer from the week. This could be about the practices, meditations, or some other way you experienced God.

After the first sharing, thank the person for sharing and return to silent prayer for a few minutes, holding the person and their words before God.

Facilitator: As we are listening to God, is there something that you want to share with _____?

Keep in mind that this is not a time to coach, give advice or tell your story. Pray over what you might say and speak from simplicity an image, verse, word, etc. that God gives you. Use your discernment, not everyone needs to share.

When the responses are over, the facilitator asks: May we pray for you aloud?

Then repeat the process until everyone has had the opportunity to share.

www.ingramcontent.com/pod-product-compliance
Lightning Source LLC
Chambersburg PA
CBHW072200100426
42738CB00011BA/2487